CAN YOU BELIEVE IT?

CAN YOU BELIEVE IT?

a hilarious collection of over 300 twisted facts to make your toes curl

Caroline West
& Mark Latter

DOG 'n' BONE

CAROLINE: For my loving family

MARK: For my Mum, how lucky was I to get you.

This edition published in 2016 by Dog 'n' Bone Books
An imprint of Ryland Peters & Small Ltd
20–21 Jockey's Fields
London WC1R 4BW

341 E 116th St
New York, NY 10029

www.rylandpeters.com

Previously published in 2015 by Dog 'n' Bone Books
under the title *OMG! Can You Believe It?*

10 9 8 7 6 5 4 3 2 1

A CIP catalog record for this book is available
from the Library of Congress and the British Library.

ISBN: 978 1 909313 92 7

Printed in China

Editor: Caroline West
Designer: Mark Latter

CONTENTS

CHAPTER 1

OMG! IT'S

OUR
HUMAN
WORLD

AMAZING
HUMAN BODY

The network of arteries, veins, and tiny capillaries in your circulatory system reach a length of approximately 60,000–100,000 miles (96,560–161,000km).

There are, amazingly, just over 37 trillion cells in the average human body.

A human thigh bone is
stronger than concrete.

* * * * * * * * * * * * * * * * * *

Achoo!
A sneeze can reach speeds of 100mph
(161km/h) as it rushes out of the mouth.
Stand back!

* * * * * * * * * * * * * * * * * *

The human heart creates
enough pressure to squirt
blood a distance
of 30ft (9m).

The lining of your stomach is replaced every 3–4 days—this is to stop strong acids digesting your own stomach.

No coughing at the back please—human coughs can travel at 60mph (97km/h).

Your nose can remember one trillion different smells.

There is enough carbon in your body to make about 9,000 pencils.

Human eyebrows renew themselves every 64 days.

HUMAN
GUNK & GOO!

In a lifetime, the average person will produce 9,000 gallons (43,000 liters) of saliva.

Over the course of a lifetime, the average human will shed 40lb (18kg) of dead skin—that's enough to fill 18 bags of sugar!

The majority of us produce about a cup of snot every day—most of this trickles unnoticed down the throat, but even so...

The average man produces around 10 million sperm cells every day.

↓↓↓↓↓↓↓↓↓↓↓↓↓↓↓↓↓↓↓↓↓↓↓↓↓↓↓↓↓↓↓

There are 250,000 sweat glands on a typical pair of feet.

↑↑↑↑↑↑↑↑↑↑↑↑↑↑↑↑↑↑↑↑↑↑↑↑↑↑↑↑↑↑↑↑

Only human beings cry tears as a result of emotion. We are also the only mammals to blush!

It takes 20 seconds for a red blood cell to travel round the whole human body.

WE ARE HUMAN TRASH CANS

Most of us love peanut butter, right? But did you know your favorite spread may contain traces of grit and up to one rodent hair per 4oz (100g)?

Obsessed with breaking world records, speed-eating legend Takeru Kobayashi managed to eat 57 pink, slimy cow brains—weighing a total of 17.7lb (8kg)—in only 15 minutes at Nathan's Hot Dog Eating Contest, which is held on Coney Island every year.

Canned mushrooms are pretty healthy, but the odd maggot is allowed to lurk in the can by the American food standards agency.

* * * * * * * * * * * *

American Donald A. Gorske likes a burger or two. Having eaten Big Macs daily throughout his life, he consumed his 26,000th Big Mac on October 11, 2012.

* * * * * * * * * * * *

On April 27, 2000, Ken Edwards from England ate 24 cooked and crunchy cockroaches in one minute on a London television show.

WEIRD WORLD FOODS

In Cambodia, people enjoy snacking on deep-fried tarantulas—including the legs and head!

Why not try some *sannakji*, or live octopus tentacles? For this Korean dish, simply cut up a wriggling octopus and then season with sesame oil and seeds. Be careful, though: the suction cups can get stuck to the inside of your mouth, tongue, teeth, and throat!

Gaeng Kai Mot Daeng, a dish popular in Thailand, combines whole ants, ant eggs, and ant larvae with spices to make a soup that tastes a bit shrimpy. Yum!

Pidan, often known as century eggs, are preserved duck eggs which are a delicacy in China. The eggs are covered with clay, ash, and salt for a few months before being dug up and eaten. The yolks go greenish-gray and the eggs stink of sulfur; still, they've been doing it for years, so they must be good, mmm?

In China and Vietnam, street vendors sell fried silkworm pupae and sea horses as a quick snack.

Casu Marzu, anyone? In Sardinia, Italy, the locals enjoy munching on a little rotten cheese. They introduce cheese fly larvae (*Piophila casei*) into Pecorino cheese to promote fermentation. As the larvae hatch out, they eat through the cheese and soften it in the process. **To eat:** dig in with a spoon and enjoy, either with or without the maggots!

MEDICAL MIRACLES

Ashik Gavai, from Buldhana in western India, experienced severe jaw pain for over a year before doctors removed 232 teeth-like growths from his mouth—this condition is known as complex odontoma.

A terrible industrial accident left a Chinese factory worker with 10 severed digits. Miraculously, surgeons were able to stitch the fingers back on in a life-changing, but grueling, operation that lasted 13 hours.

Foreskins from circumcized baby boys are used to heal burns patients and in the production of much-needed human skin for surgical procedures.

The world's youngest parents were only eight and nine years old. They lived in China in 1910.

In 2004, when Jeanna Giese was bitten by a bat in Fond-du-Lac, Wisconsin, little did she know that she had been infected with rabies. But the nightmarish symptoms of fatigue, slurred speech, and double vision started appearing a month later. She had only days to live, so her doctors pioneered an experimental treatment—known as the Milwaukee Protocol—which involved a medically induced coma. Amazingly, Jeanna survived, becoming the first person to survive rabies without ever being vaccinated.

DISTRESSING DISEASES

Mermaid Syndrome—also known as sirenomella—is a very rare medical condition in which a person is born with fused lower limbs.

During the Dance Fever Plague of 1518, hundreds of people in Strasbourg, France, danced continuously for a month without drinking, eating, or resting. Some people even danced themselves to death.

Fish Odour Syndrome. Sounds fishy? Well, read on. Sufferers of this condition have difficulty breaking down and digesting certain compounds in their food. The result is a strong fishy smell that is released in their sweat, breath, and urine.

On January 30, 1962, a laughing epidemic broke out in Tanganyika (now Tanzania), in Africa. The strange, uncontrollable laughing started with three schoolgirls giggling in their classroom and eventually affected about 1,000 people. Other symptoms included fainting, rashes, and crying fits.

↓↓↓↓↓↓↓↓↓↓↓↓↓↓↓↓↓↓↓↓↓↓↓↓↓

An unusual skin disease—known as Tree Man Syndrome—is caused by the human papillomavirus (HPV). This leads to the unfortunate victim developing tree-root-like growths on his or her skin. These woody growths are made from keratin—the protein that is found in hair and nails.

↑↑↑↑↑↑↑↑↑↑↑↑↑↑↑↑↑↑↑↑↑↑↑↑↑↑

People afflicted with hypertrichosis have abnormal amounts of hair growing on their bodies, giving rise to Werewolf Syndrome because, well, the sufferers look like hairy werewolves.

WHAT'S THAT CRAWLING

ON YOU?!

The number of bacteria living on and inside you far outnumbers your own human cells. On average, each square centimeter of human skin is home to about 1 million bacteria. Shame they don't pay rent!

Beware flesh-eating maggots! The disease known as flystrike—or myiasis, to give it its clever name—is caused by flies laying eggs in hair and wounds. When the maggots hatch out, they survive by eating the host's flesh. Flystrike usually afflicts dogs, cats, and rabbits, but humans can be victims too.

Did you know that each human plays host to a pound or two of bacteria in their intestines at all times? Hard to digest, admittedly, but these visitors help to keep us fit and healthy.

The world's longest recorded tapeworm reached a staggering length of 37ft (11m). Oh yes, and tapeworms can live for 30 years or longer in your intestines, so best spot the symptoms early on!

A typical used mattress may harbor anything between 100,000 and 10 million dust mites. Get the vacuum cleaner out!

Bed bugs are nasty parasites that live in bedding and furniture. They like nothing better than to gorge on human blood and will enjoy a 10-minute drinking session before scuttling away to hide. Scarily, bed bugs can live for a year without feeding and then come back for more!

PEEK INSIDE YOUR MAKE-UP BAG
IF YOU DARE!

There may be fish scales in your lipstick. Yep, you read that right. Some lipsticks contain fish scales—available as a by-product of large-scale, commercial herring processing—to give a lovely, shimmery sheen to some lipsticks.

Japanese scientists have found a new species of bacteria—called *Microbacterium hatanonis*—that can live in hairspray.

Want plump, luscious-looking lips? Well, that's fine if you're happy to put pepper spray on your face, as many lip-plumping cosmetics contain *Oleoresin capsicum* (aka pepper spray).

Human foreskin cells are sometimes used in cosmetic creams to help reduce wrinkles.

Snail slime contains glycolic acid and elastin, which help protect snails' skin from bacteria, cuts, and UV light. The slime is also used in some moisturizers to rejuvenate skin cells.

Looking for a product to treat dry, damaged hair? Then try a hair mask containing some animal placenta for the strong, glossy hair you've always yearned for!

RANDOM RECORD BREAKERS

Annie Hawkins-Turner from Atlanta, Georgia, in the USA, has the biggest natural breasts on record, measuring a titillating 70in (177.8cm) around the nipple line. This makes her bra size an outrageous 102ZZZ.

Elaine Davidson is the world's most pierced woman. According to Guinness World Records Elaine had a total of 6,925 piercings by February 2011. There are 192 in her face alone!

The longest ever fingernails on a woman belong to Lee Redmond. Lee started growing her nails in 1979—by February 23, 2008, they had reached a combined length of 28ft 4.5in (8.65m). The longest nails grown by a man belonged to the late Melvin Booth, whose nails reached a combined length of 32ft 3.8in (9.85m).

The world's tallest living man is Sultan Kösen (born December 10, 1982). He's 8ft 3in (2.51m) tall!

* ✳ * ✳ * ✳ * ✳ * ✳ * ✳ * ✳ *

The biggest win in Las Vegas?
Turning US$50 (£32) in 1992 into over
US$40 million (£26 million) in 1995...
before losing it a year later.
Words cannot describe that pain!

* ✳ * ✳ * ✳ * ✳ * ✳ * ✳ * ✳ *

The largest pizza produced to order is made by Big Mama's & Papa's Pizzeria in Los Angeles. Measuring 4½ x 4½ft (1.37 x 1.37m), this square whopper serves 50–100 people and costs over US$200 (£131).

YOU PAID
HOW MUCH?!

In 1969 Richard Burton paid an eye-watering amount of money for a 69.42-carat diamond for his wife Elizabeth Taylor. The Taylor-Burton diamond, as it has become known, was bought by Burton for around US$1.1 million (£720,000).

A Holstein cow called Mist from East Montpelier, Vermont, was sold at auction for US$1.3 million (£850,000). She was bought by a group of investors, but still ...

Did you know that it cost US$7.5 million (£5 million)—in today's money—to build the great ship *Titanic* in 1912 and an amazing US$200 million (£130 million) to make the 1997 blockbuster film?

Pricey Animals!

- **RACEHORSE:** Green Monkey sold at auction in 2006 for US$16 million (£10.5 million)

- **DOG:** Big Splash was bought in February 2011 for US$1.5 million (£985,000)

- **FISH:** A blue fin tuna sold at Tokyo's Tsukiji fish market in 2011 for a staggering US$396,000 (£260,000)

- **SHEEP:** Deveronvale Perfection was sold in 2009 for US$352,000 (£230,000)

- **BEETLE:** A stag beetle was sold in Japan for US$89,000 (£58,000)

- **CAT:** Cato, a Bengal cat, was bought in 1998 for US$41,435 (£27,000)

CRAZY
HUMAN
LAWS

Skateboarding after dark within the city limits is prohibited in Akron, Ohio.

Adultery is officially a felony in over 20 US states, including Illinois, Minnesota, Virginia, Oklahoma, Idaho, and Wisconsin.

Inter-racial marriages were banned in South Africa from 1949 to 1985—that's a period of 36 years. They were still banned in various US states from 1664 to 2000—that's a total of 336 years!

In Alaska, a local law makes it illegal to whisper in someone's ear while they are hunting moose.

Until very recently, throwing a frisbee at the beach in Los Angeles, California—without asking the lifeguard's permission first—was prohibited.

* * * * * * * * * * * *

In Vermont, women need written permission from their husbands if they wish to wear false teeth.

* * * * * * * * * * * *

The State of Kansas requests pedestrians crossing highways at night to wear tail-lights.

MUSEUMS OF THE
WEIRD, WONDERFUL,
AND DOWNRIGHT ODD

The Parasite Museum, in Tokyo, is home to 300 different varieties of parasite. Star attractions include a parasite-infested dolphin stomach and a 30ft (9m) tapeworm that a woman apparently "invited in" after eating some sushi.

* * * * * * * * * * *

Galileo's middle finger is on display in the Museo Galileo, in Florence. (His index finger, thumb, and tooth are now there, too.)

* * * * * * * * * * *

The Icelandic Phallological Museum
contains a collection of penises
of various shapes and sizes, from
the huge member of a blue whale
to the tiny appendages of mice
and shrews. This is all done in
the name of science, of course—
phallology, apparently.

Amsterdam is famous
for a lot of things, but did you know that
it has a Torture Museum? Enter its doors,
if you dare, and discover rusty old
guillotines, crushing screws, and
stretching tables.

Housed rather appropriately
underground, Barcelona's Museum of
Funeral Carriages is an eerie guide
to previous generations' attitudes
to death—as far back as the 18th
century. Seeing is probably
believing in this instance.

FACTS TO MAKE
YOU THINK

Most people use computers, right? Well, here are some of the things that are probably trapped in your keyboard: old food, hair, dandruff, saliva, dead skin cells, and body fat. This leads to infestations from bacteria, viruses, and other microbes!

At the time you were born, you were very, very briefly the youngest person in the world.

The Bible is the most shoplifted book in the United States.

A packet of Wrigley's Juicy Fruit chewing gum was the first product with a barcode to be scanned in June 1974.

Months that begin on a Sunday always have a Friday 13th.

You'd think the sound effects would be part of a film's multi-million-dollar budget, wouldn't you? Well, some of the dinosaur sounds in the 1993 movie *Jurassic Park* were created using recordings of tortoises having sex.

RANDOM
FAMOUS
PEOPLE FACTS

Like all of us, Alfred Hitchcock was born with a belly button, but he had it sewn up surgically! Don't ask why, as we don't know!

$E=mc^2$ and all that, but did you know that for some reason Albert Einstein never wore any socks?

Nazi leader Adolf Hitler had only one testicle.

Walt Disney was afraid of mice... poor Mickey Mouse!

* * * * * * * * * * * * * * * *

Thomas Edison—who invented reliable electric light bulbs—was afraid of the dark. Apparently, he had all the lights on in his house when he died.

Agatha Christie enjoyed surfing.

Ambidextrous Leonardo da Vinci could simultaneously write forward with one hand and backward with the other. Leonardo was also the first person to explain why the sky is blue—he was, clearly, a man of many talents.

CHAPTER 2

OMG! IT'S

THE
ANIMAL
KINGDOM

MAMMAL MARVELS

The blue whale (*Balaenoptera musculus*) has a heart that weighs about half a tonne and blood vessels wide enough for a human to swim through. Not surprisingly, baby blue whales need to drink up to 50 gallons (227 liters) of milk a day to get that big!

Hungry as a jackal? Jackals aren't fussy eaters and will happily tuck into decomposing or diseased meat. The pups have even been known to eat their mother's vomit. Waste not, want not...

Air can escape from the lungs
of a hedgehog and become
trapped under its skin, making
it blow up like a balloon.
The afflicted animal has to
be carefully deflated with
a syringe before it bursts.

In one year, a colony of around 100 common vampire
bats (*Desmodus rotundus*) can consume the blood of
25 cows. They need to feed on blood nearly every day
in order to survive and will drink their victim's blood
for about 30 minutes at each sitting (or should we
say biting). These bats sometimes like a little
tipple from humans, too. Sleep tight!

Camels have three
eyelids to protect
their eyes from blowing
desert sands and dust.

Weirdly, nine-banded armadillos (*Dasypus novemcinctus*) nearly always give birth to a set of identical quadruplets—of the same sex. Strangely, armadillos are also the only animals apart from humans that can get leprosy.

Pigs and hippopotamuses get sunburn. Clever hippos, however, secrete an oily red substance over their skin that acts as a moisturizer and sunblock.

Giraffes pick their noses too! Using their 18–20in (45–50cm) tongues, these elegant creatures are still not averse to having a good dig around in their nostrils. Female giraffes also give birth while standing up, which means the unfortunate baby has to drop around 6ft (1.8m) to the ground.

Chilling Rat Facts

➜ Rats can carry a host of nasty diseases, including salmonella, tuberculosis, Weil's disease, and foot and mouth diseases.

➜ About 4,000 rats are born every hour in London alone.

➜ A female rat will mate up to 500 times over a six-hour period and a pair of brown rats (*Rattus norvegicus*) can produce as many as 2,000 furry relatives in a year.

➜ These determined rodents can tread water for three days and survive being flushed down a toilet—did we mention that they then get back into the building using the same unsanitary route?

➜ Perhaps the most mind-blowing rat fact, though, is that a rat's teeth are coated with enamel stronger than a human's, so they can gnaw through masonry and metal.

➜ Scarily, studies suggest that disease-carrying rats are developing resistance to the poisons we commonly use to kill them.

True story: In 2014, a massive rat measuring 16in (40cm) in length—and that's not including its tail—and weighing 2.2lb (1kg) was captured and killed in a home in Stockholm, Sweden.

POOCHES
AND OTHER PETS

Dog urine can corrode metal—in fact, doggy pee nonchalantly aimed at the base of lamp posts has been blamed for a number of them collapsing in Zagreb, Croatia.

A dog's nose print is as individual as a human fingerprint.

Many hamsters blink only one eye at a time.

Dogs can be pretty smart—border collies, for example, can understand up to 200 words. Amazingly, a border collie called Chaser from South Carolina in the US knows just over 1,000 words.

Owing to inbreeding, three out of 10 Dalmatian dogs have hearing loss.

A dog's sense of smell is 1,000 to 10,000 times greater than ours.

Like Caucasian human babies, all kittens are born with blue eyes.

Cats are either right- or left-pawed— just like us!

BIRDS BEAUTIFUL AND OTHERWISE

Birds living in cities have discovered that lining their nests with cigarette butts deters parasites. Apparently, the burnt nicotine works like an insecticide and helps ward off mites, lice, and fleas.

Cave swiftlets (*Collocalia linchi*) line their nests with saliva and pre-digested seaweed to form a hard, translucent layer, so creating a strong nest. Did you know these are the same nests used to make bird's nest soup?

The red-billed oxpecker (*Buphagus erythrorhynchus*) is beautiful, but take a look at its diet—top of the menu are blood, ticks, rotting flesh, dandruff, and earwax. Dessert anyone?

> Nightingales can remember
> up to 200 different songs.

Miracle Mike was a Wyandotte chicken that managed to survive for 18 months after his head had been chopped off with an axe. Born in April 1945, Mike lost his head aged about five and a half months, when farmer Lloyd Olsen went out to kill a chicken for supper. Unfortunately for Mike, the axe missed his jugular and left most of his brain stem intact. Poor Mike survived on milk and water served from an eyedropper and tiny grains of corn—fed to him by his, no doubt, guilty owner. Mike even attempted to crow, as before, but only managed to emit a gurgling sound in his throat. OMG!

Woodpeckers can peck up to 20 times per second—that's around 8,000–12,000 pecks a day.

The turkey vulture (*Cathartes aura*) defecates and pees all over its legs. This nasty habit serves a useful purpose, though, since the water evaporating from the feces helps the vulture cool down. The acidic pee also kills off any bacteria the bird might have picked up hopping over its dead-animal supper.

REPULSIVE
REPTILES AND
AMPHIBIANS

The Texas horned lizard (*Phrynosoma cornutum*) has a crazy way of defending itself when its sharp spikes and horns don't do the trick. This lizard can squirt a stream of blood from its eyes. The blood can travel as much as 5ft (1.5m) and is mixed with a nasty-smelling chemical to keep predators at bay.

The Komodo dragon (*Varanus komodoensis*) is the largest lizard on Earth. It has the bizarre (but actually quite sensible) habit of shaking its prey backward and forward to release the poo from the animal's intestines before eating. Baby dragons also roll around in poo as a way of warding off predators—including adult dragons, which have been known to cannibalize their young.

A chameleon can move its eyes in two directions at the same time.

The king cobra (*Ophiophagus hannah*) hisses a warning before striking. That's pretty useful, actually, as the quantity of neurotoxin it can inject with one bite is enough to kill one elephant or 20 humans. (Incidentally, the king cobras used by snake charmers cannot actually hear the music being played to them, but are attracted by the movement of the flute.)

The golden poison frog (*Phyllobates terribilis*) is regarded (not surprisingly, given its Latin name) as one of the most toxic animals on Earth, containing enough venom to kill 10 adults.

BUGS AND
BEASTIES

Ant invasion! Scientists have unearthed a single mega colony of Argentine ants (*Linepithema humile*) that covers three continents: part of Europe, the west coast of the US, and the west coast of Japan. In spite of the huge distances between them, ants from the different areas acted as if they knew one another in scientific trials. Just one big happy ant family!

The giant African millipede grows to 15in (38cm) in length, while *Crurifarcimen vagans* is the largest millipede native to Tanzania—this one's also more curiously known as the wandering leg sausage.

Tear-drinking bees. Yep, you read that right: there is a species of bee that will feed on human sweat and even drink human tears!

Cockroaches appeared on Earth before the first dinosaurs. They are clearly made of strong stuff, as a cockroach can live for several weeks with its head cut off and some species can survive without air for 45 minutes. Perhaps the scariest cockroach of all is the American cockroach (*Periplaneta americana*), which feeds on human hair, eyelashes, eyebrows, and toenails.

Ants don't have enough mass to die on impact, no matter what height they fall from.

Vampire jumping spiders from East Africa are attracted to the smell of human feet.

The babies of the black lace-weaver spider (*Amaurobius ferox*) eat their mother's body as soon as they hatch out of their eggs. Motherly love, eh?

The Giant African land snail can reach an incredible, squishy length of 8in (20cm).

In the United States, banana slugs, which are often yellow in color—hence their name—can grow to 12in (30cm) in length and have up to 27,000 toothy protrusions on a tongue-like radula to grind up their food.

Slugs are gastropods, which means "stomach foot" in Greek. Nice.

The average garden in the
United Kingdom is home to
a population of around
20,000 slugs.

Slugs leave an individual
scent trail so that they can
find their way back home.

Slugs are able to stretch
to 20 times their usual
length—meaning they can
make a quick getaway
through cracks and holes.

Snails are superheroes—they can lift up
to 10 times their own body weight.

FREAKY FISH AND SEA CREATURES

Some North Atlantic lobsters (*Homarus americanus*) are born blue because of a rare genetic defect.

Some species of turtle—notably the North American eastern painted turtle (*Chrysemys picta*)—can breathe out of their bottoms.

Octopuses have three hearts, blue blood, rectangular pupils, and fantastic color vision. They are also pretty clever—octopuses in captivity have been observed playing with little toys as they drift in the water in the aquarium. If that isn't amazing enough, octopuses also like to collect bottle caps, pretty stones, and other items from the bottom of the sea to decorate their dens.

Anglerfish have a black-lined stomach. This is so that they don't give themselves away if they've eaten something luminous.

A sea cucumber will vomit up or defecate its own internal organs to act as a distraction when threatened by a predator. The sea cucumber can then make a dash for it and escape. Don't worry, though, sea cucumbers are echinoderms, which means that they can easily grow replacement organs.

Whale sharks (*Rhincodon typus*) lay the largest eggs in the world—an egg found in the Gulf of Mexico in 1953 had a diameter of 14in (35cm).

Jellyfish have been living on Earth for over 650 million years. The largest jellyfish in the world is the lion's mane jellyfish (*Cyanea capillata*)—one recorded specimen had tentacles measuring a jaw-dropping 120ft (37m).

ANIMALS UNDER ATTACK

When swallowing prey, such as crickets, the Northern leopard frog (*Lithobates pipiens*) retracts its eyes to help push the food down its throat. Apparently, this is a retraction and swallowing technique—must be quite a sight!

Electric eels can use a built-in taser to stun their prey from a distance. Along with two organs situated on the abdomen that deliver low-voltage pulses to help the eel "see" its surroundings, scientists have discovered a third organ which supplies a high-voltage pulse that immobilizes prey in milliseconds.

When under attack, the hairy frog (*Trichobatrachus robustus*) from Central Africa breaks the toe bones in its feet and then forces the splintered shards through the skin in order to stab its attacker. Horror frog!

Hagfish are eel-shaped sea creatures that get out of a tight corner by releasing slime from their pores. The slime expands into a jelly-like goo when it comes into contact with water, leaving the poor predator trapped, choking, or suffocated.

A species of termite found in the rainforests of French Guiana sends out older termites to defend the colony when it's under attack. These sacrificial termites carry explosive "backpacks," which fill up over their lifetime with toxic blue crystals that are produced by glands in their abdomens. When mixed with saliva from a biting predator, the crystals produce a toxic blue venom that explodes all over the attacker. Although the predator is only paralyzed, the poor termite dies heroically defending the colony.

SORRY, I JUST CAN'T!

Unlike most members of the cat family, cheetahs cannot fully retract their claws.

Hummingbirds are amazing acrobats of the air, but have poorly developed feet, so they can barely walk or hop.

Horses can't vomit—most likely because they have a one-way valve at the top of their stomachs.

A kangaroo can't jump unless its tail is touching the ground.

Guinea pigs and rabbits can't sweat.

The only breed of dog that can't bark is the Basenji. They can growl, whine, chuckle, and scream, though.

Neither kangaroos nor emus can walk backward.

Armadillos, opossums, and sloths can't stay awake, spending up to 80 percent of their lives asleep.

A crocodile cannot stick out its tongue.

CHAPTER 3

OMG! IT'S

THE NAUGHTY BITS

SSSHHHHHH!

HUMANS

Humans can burn off 200 calories if they have sex for about 30 minutes.

Humans are the only species that have sex purely for pleasure—apart from dolphins and bonobos (*Pan paniscus*), which are a type of chimpanzee.

British spies experimented with using semen as an invisible ink during the First World War! Rather ironically, the man who pioneered the technique was called Mansfield Cumming. The semen had to be fresh, though, as some correspondents complained about receiving smelly letters.

Sex can work as a painkiller and even help cure a severe headache—ironic, really, given that having a headache is often cited as a reason for not wanting to have sex in the first place.

Your inner nose swells during sexual intercourse, along with other more obvious parts of the anatomy.

On Valentine's Day, 2013, a couple broke the record for kissing for the longest time without stopping—they managed to snog for a draining 58 hours, 35 minutes, and 58 seconds.

! ! ! ! ! ! ! ! ! ! ! ! ! ! ! !

Sneezes—as well as orgasms, obviously—are the only physiological responses that you cannot control voluntarily once they have started.

! ! ! ! ! ! ! ! ! ! ! ! ! ! ! !

Heard of the Mile High Club? Here are a few figures to intrigue you: when surveyed, the following nationals admitted to being members—French (27 percent), Germans (18 percent), and British (11 percent), with the Italians (6 percent), Americans, and Spanish (both on 4 percent) lagging a little behind.

JUST FOR THE BOYS

The first sperm banks opened in Tokyo and Iowa City in 1965.

The average man reaches his reproductive peak at around 18. Then, it's down hill all the way.

Sperm wasn't discovered until 1677 when Dutch microscope maker Antonie van Leeuwenhoek revealed seeing "little animals" moving about like eels under his microscope lens.

Men ejaculate at an average speed of 28mph (45km/h). With nothing in the way, the male penis can squirt semen a distance of 12–24in (30–60cm).

The longest erect penis on record measured 13.5in (34cm) and belonged to American Jonah Falcon. The smallest erect penis measured only ½in (1cm).

The majority of men living in the US have been circumcized.

A teaspoon of semen contains about 5–25 calories and 400 million sperm. Sperm make up only one percent of semen, however—the rest is comprised of water, citric acid, enzymes, proteins, and potassium, among other substances. Quite a cocktail, then.

JUST FOR THE GIRLS

Did you know that the infamous G-spot was once called the Whipple Tickle?

Squalene is a natural lubricant found in the vagina—believe it or not, this substance is also found in shark livers.

Vaginas can fall out! Yep, that's correct: in a medical condition called pelvic organ prolapse, the uterus, vagina, bowel, and bladder move out of position—and, in extreme cases, the vagina may appear outside the body. Panic not, as the condition can be fixed.

The clitoris contains 8,000 nerve endings, while the penis has only 4,000.

The rising popularity of Brazilian waxes has led to a reduction in the pubic-lice population.

The most female orgasms ever recorded in an hour was an amazing 134.

CONTRACEPTION
AND BIRTH

The Ancient Egyptians used crocodile dung as a contraceptive—no one knows who pioneered the technique.

Cave paintings dating back
to 10,000–13,000 BC in
Les Combarelles, in the Dordogne,
southern France, clearly depict
a man using an early condom.

In the mid-1980s, some very old condoms were found in the cesspit at Dudley Castle, England. Thought to date back to the 1640s, they were made from fish and animal intestines.

We have all heard how eating a curry, drinking raspberry leaf tea, and having sex can bring on labor in pregnant women, but, apparently, rubbing or rolling a woman's nipples when full term can stimulate the release of a hormone called oxytocin, which causes contractions.

In May 2010, a baby boy was born from a frozen embryo that was 20 years old.

Between 1725 and 1765 a Russian peasant woman gave birth to 69 children— her family included 16 sets of twins, seven sets of triplets, and four sets of quadruplets. OMG!

According to Guinness World Records, the longest interval between the birth of twins to the same mother is 87 days.

BIZARRE PHOBIAS AND FETISHES

Scared to look in the mirror in the morning? Then you may be afflicted with spectrophobia.

A fear of the color purple is known as porphyrophobia.

Being scared of birds makes you ornithophobic.

Pteronophobia is the fear of being tickled with feathers.

Being frightened of slime means that you're suffering from blennophobia.

Toilet issues—people frightened of being constipated have coprastasophobia.

Some Strange
Sexual Fetishes

🌹 FORMICHOPHILIA: The enjoyment of insects crawling over or nibbling you for sexual pleasure.

🌹 FLATULOPHILIA: Being aroused by someone else farting—nice one that.

🌹 SYMPHOROPHILIA: An attraction to disasters such as fires, traffic accidents, and hurricanes.

🌹 MUCOPHILIA: Being turned on by mucus and snot, so best to avoid those with blennophobia (see opposite).

🌹 DENDROPHILIA: A sexual interest in trees.

🌹 TRICHOPHILIA: An attraction to hair.

🌹 HYBRISTOPHILIA: Attraction to very violent and dangerous criminals. The syndrome is popularly known as the Bonnie and Clyde Syndrome.

🌹 MECHANOPHILIA: Being sexually attracted to cars or other machines.

🌹 AGALMATOPHILIA: A fetishistic attraction to dolls, statues, and mannequins.

ANIMAL SEX

There is a species of praying mantis—*Mantis religiosa*—in which sex can be more efficient if the male's head is severed from his body first. So, the female mantis sometimes initiates sex by ripping the male's head off.

A species of sea slug—*Goniobranchus reticulatus*—severs its own penis after mating and then promptly grows a new one for next time.

Dogs can remain locked together for 15–20 minutes after copulating, with the male's member trapped securely inside the female's vagina.

A species of tropical spider called *Nephilengys malabarensis* uses penis-like organs called palps to transfer sperm to the female. This is a dangerous time for the male, though, as it's then that the female may grab him for supper. To avoid this nasty fate, the male spider detaches one of his two palps and leaves it attached to the female to finish off the job, while he makes a quick getaway.

Wild boar ejaculate for a period of 5–10 minutes—it takes so long because the boar produces 17 fl oz (500ml) of semen per ejaculation.

According to Guinness World Records, the male scaly cricket (*Ornebius aperta*) from Australia can have sex more than 50 times in three to four hours—all with the same female. Leaving nothing to chance, then.

EXTREME ANIMAL APPENDAGES

Echidna penises have four cup-shaped heads at the end. So, there must be an evolutionary reason for this, right? Well, maybe so, but it all sounds a bit complicated, as two of the heads need to shrink away and the other two rotate before mating can take place. What a palaver!

Female kangaroos have three vaginas and two wombs. Apparently, this complex set-up enables kangaroos to be pregnant permanently—the female kangaroo can simultaneously have an embryo developing in one of her wombs and a tiny joey in her pouch.

In spotted hyenas, the male penis and female clitoris look extraordinarily similar. Confusingly, female hyenas also have a fused vulva that resembles a fat-filled scrotal sack. As a result, the female hyena has to pee, mate, and give birth through her clitoris (or pseudo-penis). Confused? So are we!

The male and female of a species of marmoset—*Mico saterei*—have developed bright orange genitalia. Both sexes have long, fleshy, labia-like appendages framing their usual sex organs—some sort of advertisement, maybe?

Not many birds have penises, but the Argentine lake duck (*Oxyura vittata*) does—and it's weird! The penis of this small duck is shaped like a corkscrew and is almost 3ft (1m) in length.

CHAPTER 4

OMG! IT'S

THE
WORLD
AROUND
US

AWESOME
SPACE FACTS

Astrophysicists think that only around five percent of the matter in the Universe is visible. The other 95 percent is composed of invisible dark matter and dark energy.

A manned space rocket can travel to the Moon more quickly than a stagecoach could travel the length of England.

Scientists believe there are 10 times more stars in the night sky than grains of sand on the world's beaches and deserts. There are 70 thousand million million million stars visible from Earth through telescopes.

Over the last 20 years, NASA space shuttles have achieved the following: carried 3 million pounds (1.36 million kilograms) of cargo, transported more than 600 pilots and passengers, spent a total of three years in flight, and traveled more than 366 million miles (589 million kilometers).

Astronauts in space are allowed a selection of condiments with their food, including salt and pepper, taco sauce, hot pepper sauce, ketchup, mustard, and mayonnaise.

Buzz Aldrin was the second man to set foot on the Moon (Neil Armstrong got there just before him), but the first to urinate there once he'd arrived—in his spacesuit, of course!

Most of the elements in the human body originated in the stars.

The Soviet Zond 5 spacecraft launched into space in 1968. Onboard were seeds, plants, bacteria, worms, and flies—plus two Russian tortoises that became the first animals to orbit the Moon.

Alan Shepard is the only person to have hit a golf ball on the Moon. On February 6, 1971, during the Apollo 14 space mission, Shepard hit two golf balls using a golf-club head and balls that he'd smuggled onboard.

They are still there to this day.

Amazing
Planet Facts

✳ **MERCURY:** Scientists have discovered that "wrinkles" formed on the surface of this planet, as its iron core cooled and contracted. Known as lobate scarps, these wrinkles can be up to a mile high and hundreds of miles long. Mercury is also the most cratered planet in the Solar System, being scarred by numerous impacts with asteroids and comets.

✳ **VENUS:** This is one hell of a holiday destination— brace yourself, as the surface temperature reaches 864°F (462°C) and the air pressure is 92 times greater than here on Earth (meaning you'd be crushed to death). Oh yes, and best to point out that the lovely white clouds that drift around this planet are made from sulfuric acid and the wind blows at a superfast 186mph (300km/h).

✳ **URANUS:** This icy giant has 27 moons (and counting). Rather touchingly, these are named after characters from the works of William Shakespeare and Alexander Pope, including Shakespeare's Oberon, Titania, and Puck and Pope's Belinda, Ariel, and Umbriel.

✳ **EARTH:** Did you know that this is the only planet in our Solar System that is not named after a god?

※ **MARS:** Heard of the mighty Olympus Mons? Well, it's the tallest mountain in the Solar System—and probably actively volcanic—with a height of 13 miles (21km) and a diameter of 373 miles (600km).

※ **JUPITER:** So huge is this monster planet that you could fit 1,000 Earths inside it. Jupiter's famous Great Red Spot is a huge storm that has been thundering away for at least 350 years.

※ **SATURN:** It's raining diamonds on Saturn and Jupiter! Apparently, lightning storms turn methane gas into carbon, which hardens into pieces of graphite and then diamond "hail stones" as it falls.

※ **NEPTUNE:** This beautiful blue planet has 14 moons and very wild weather, with large storms swirling in the upper atmosphere and furiously fast winds traveling at a mind-boggling 656 yards/sec (600m/sec).

※ **PLUTO:** Happily spinning at the very edges of our Solar System, this icy rock is unaware of the controversy that surrounds it. It was identified in 1930 as the ninth planet orbiting our Sun, but scientists reclassified it as a dwarf planet in 2006. However, recent images taken by the Hubble Space Telescope suggest that Pluto is, in fact, a proper planet (albeit a small one). Soon NASA's New Horizons space probe will fly by Pluto to take some measurements and count its moons. Then, hopefully, there will be a final decision on Pluto's status.

AMAZING
EARTH FACTS

Reykjavik, in Iceland, is the world's most northerly capital city, while the southernmost is Wellington, New Zealand. These capitals are a staggering 10,700 miles (17,000km) apart.

Supersonic flight! When flying from London to New York by Concorde, you would have arrived two hours before you left owing to the difference in time zones.

The Amazon rainforest provides about 20 percent of the world's oxygen.

A flow of salt water contaminated with iron oxide, which oozes from the Taylor Glacier in east Antarctica, is known as Blood Falls because it looks as though the ice is bleeding.

Diamonds boil at 8,700°F (4,827°C).

WILD
WEATHER

In 1899, the weather was so cold that the Mississippi River froze over completely—for its entire length.

The wettest place on Earth is Mawsynram in the Khasi Hills, north-east India—receiving 467in (11.86m) of rain a year. It rains there almost continuously.

The hottest temperature ever recorded on Earth was a searing 134°F (56.7°C) at Greenland Ranch, in Death Valley, California, on July 10, 1913.

The largest snowflakes ever recorded fell during a storm in January 1887 at Fort Keogh, Montana, USA. Some flakes measured 15in (45cm) in diameter.

The largest recorded hailstone hit the ground during a massive storm in Vivian, South Dakota, USA; it had a diameter of 8in (20cm)—that's about the size of a small soccer ball.

Rain has never been recorded falling in some parts of the Atacama Desert, Chile.

Meteorologists estimate that there are around 1,800 thunderstorms taking place somewhere over the surface of the Earth at any given moment.

The coldest temperature recorded on Earth was a bone-numbing -135.8°F (-94.7°C) in east Antarctica in August 2010.

SHAKE, RATTLE, AND ROLL

A tornado that devastated Oklahoma City in May 1999 reached a record-breaking wind speed of 318mph (512km/h). On average, about 60 people a year die as a result of tornadoes in the United States.

In March 1925, a devastating tornado swept across Missouri, Illinois, and Indiana, killing 695 people and injuring 2,027 others. However, the world's deadliest tornado occurred in Bangladesh in April 1989—killing around 1,300 and leaving many thousands homeless.

Krakatoa, a volcano in the Sunda Strait between Sumatra and Java, last erupted in August 1883, exploding with the loudest sound ever heard. The eruption and ensuing tsunami killed around 36,000 people. Unbelievably, the explosion could be heard 3,000 miles (4,800km) away and affected global weather patterns for years.

The worst volcanic eruption of modern times took place on April 10, 1815, when Mount Tambora erupted on Sumbawa Island, Indonesia, claiming the lives of 92,000 people. This explosion was around 100 times more violent than the 1980 eruption of Mount St Helens, in California—just to note: the energy produced by St Helens was equal to 2,500 nuclear bombs.

Shattering Earthquakes

★ **1556**: The deadliest earthquake on record took place on January 23, 1556, in the Shaanxi Province of northwest China. It killed over 800,000 people.

★ **1920**: On December 18, 1920, in Haiyuan County, China, a massive earthquake, measuring 8.5 on the Richter scale, devastated the area. The death toll was over 270,000.

★ **1960**: The world's most powerful recorded earthquake rocked Chile on May 22, 1960. Miraculously, the quake (measuring an astounding 9.5 on the Richter scale) and resulting 30ft-high (10m) tsunami killed only about 2,000 people. However, the disaster destroyed entire villages and left two million people homeless.

★ **1976**: This year is remembered as "the year of the curse" in Tangshan, China, because a savage earthquake, with a magnitude of 7.8, reduced the city to rubble on July 28. There is controversy as to how many people lost their lives, but suffice to say most of the city was flattened.

★ **2004**: Who can forget the earthquake that shook the Indian Ocean on Boxing Day 2004? As the floor of the ocean cracked open, a 100ft-high (30m) tsunami swept through Indonesia, Thailand, India, and even parts of eastern Africa. All in all, 14 countries were affected and around 250,000 people died.

★ **2008**: China's Sichuan Province was preparing for the 2008 Beijing Olympics when a 7.9-magnitude earthquake ripped through the area on May 12. Over 65,000 people were killed and a further 18,000 were listed as missing. All in all, some 5 million people were left homeless.

★ **2010**: On January 12, 2010, a massive earthquake measuring 7.0 on the Richter scale devastated the Caribbean island nation of Haiti. The earth-shattering quake claimed the lives of more than 230,000 people.

CURIOUS
COUNTRIES

Japan has lactation bars that supply human breast milk. For US$17 (£11), you can get a nice shot of milk— US$42(£27) procures a nipple too!

In Germany, people used to pile their household poo in front of their homes. Apparently, the bigger the pile of poo, the wealthier you were seen to be!

Chess is compulsory for primary-school children in Armenia.

More than 30 million people live in caves in China, particularly in Shaanxi Province, where the porous soil makes it easier to excavate into the side of mountains.

The Alaskan flag, with its bright blue background and eight gold stars, was designed by a 13-year-old boy called Bennie Benson in a flag-designing competition in 1927.

Switzerland is the land of snow-clad mountains, delicious chocolate, and super-accurate watches, right? Well, consider these facts: men joining the military (it's compulsory at the age of 19) are required by law to take their weapons home once they are discharged, and the country is riddled with bomb shelters—because, since 1963, every household must build one in case of nuclear attack. So, you know where to head if the sirens go off!

Russia has a larger surface area than Pluto.

Saudi Arabia imports live camels from Australia. They are transported in ships that are specially designed to accommodate camels.

CRAZY CITIES

Birmingham, UK, has more miles of canals than Venice, Italy. It also has more trees than Paris.

The mouth of New York's iconic Statue of Liberty is 3ft (90cm) wide!

There is a town in Pennsylvania, USA, called Intercourse, and one in West Virginia known as Looneyville!

Parts of Mexico City are sinking at a rate of 4in (10cm) per year—that's about 10 times faster than Venice, Italy.

There is a National Museum of Pasta in Rome, Italy.

Chefchaouen, in the Rif Mountains of Morocco, is quite a tourist attraction—because the white-washed buildings are painted in shades of blue.

New York is home to the Empire State Building and the United Nations, but did you know Brooklyn also plays host to a population of bright green quaker parrots? It seems that these tropical visitors escaped at JFK Airport from a shipment originating in South America.

There are just over 800,000 people living within the city limits of Amsterdam, but it's estimated that there are about 1,000,000 bicycles.

RANDOM
PLANT FACTS

Carrots were originally purple or white rather than orange. If you feel the need to discover more about this vegetable staple, then check out the virtual World Carrot Museum.

Human DNA is over 95% identical to that of chimpanzees. Sure, we hear you say, that makes sense, but did you know that we also share 50% of our DNA with bananas?

The titan arum (*Amorphophallus titanum*) grows in the rainforests of western Sumatra, Indonesia. It is nicknamed the corpse flower because its incredibly huge flower stinks of dead and decomposing animals in order to attract pollinating insects. The plant's giant, phallus-like flowering structure is the tallest in the world, too, rising some 10ft (3m) above the ground.

Often labeled as one of the world's ugliest plants, the tree tumbo (*Welwitschia mirabilis*) is found in the Namibian desert. Specimens can live for over 2,000 years and have leaves that grow up to 20ft (6m) long. This fascinating plant supplies desert mammals with moisture and nutrients, as well as providing snakes and lizards with some shelter from the blazing sun.

Strawberries aren't really berries, but avocadoes, pumpkins, and bananas are.

Here's another nauseating plant! The stinking corpse lily (*Rafflesia arnoldii*) reeks of rotting flesh. This charmer parasitizes rainforest vines and sucks out their juices. The single, huge, orangey-brown flower—which can grow up to 3ft (90cm) across and weighs an amazing 2.2lb (1kg)—has leathery petals covered in warts. Pollinating insects find these floral beauties irresistible, apparently.

The calabash tree (*Crescentia cujete*) from Central America is pollinated by bats. For this reason, it has large, pale, night-flowering blossoms that give off an aroma of sweaty cheese to entice the bats!

CHAPTER 5

OMG! IT'S

ADVENTURE AND SURVIVAL

I'M IN FREE FALL!

While attempting a 10,000ft (3,000m) skydive, Paul Lewis's parachute failed to open and he went into free fall. Luckily, Paul landed on a hangar roof at Tilstock Airfield, Shropshire, England.

The rollercoaster with the longest, fastest, and biggest drop is the Daidarasaurus, in Nagashima Spa Land, Japan. If you fancy a ride, please note: the drop is 307ft (93.5m) and the top speed 95mph (153km/h).

When a bomber hit the 79th floor of the Empire State Building, New York, on July 28, 1945, no one imagined that elevator operator Betty Lou Oliver would survive. She was suffering from burns and rescue crews put her in an elevator so she could receive immediate medical attention. But the elevator cables were so badly damaged that they snapped, sending Oliver into free fall. Amazingly, she survived and went back to work five months later—in the same elevator!

Tricky things, parachutes! This is what Lyndi Harding discovered to her horror in California in April 2001 when she leaped from a plane at 8,500ft (2,600m)—and her parachute failed to open. Lyndi fell through the air for 40 seconds, traveling at a speed of 70mph (113km/h). She sustained fractured ribs, a punctured lung, a broken nose, and a chipped tooth—but lived to tell the tale.

In 2007, brothers Alcides and Edgar Moreno were cleaning the windows of a New York apartment block. The cable securing the cleaning platform suddenly snapped and the pair plummeted 500ft (152m) to the ground. By some miracle, Alcides survived the fall—although he was left in a coma with multiple fractures—and made a complete recovery. Sadly, his brother Edgar wasn't so lucky.

American Sam Patch liked to jump off things. In October 1829, he leaped 120ft (37m) from Niagara Falls and survived. Gaining confidence, Patch then jumped from the River Genesee's Upper Falls, in Rochester, New York. For some bizarre reason, he made the jump with a pet bear cub! A week later, on Friday 13th—didn't he think?!—he attempted the jump again, but without the bear. This time, "The Yankee Leaper," as he became known, did not survive.

ALL AT SEA

1942: On November 23, merchant seaman Poon Lim jumped overboard when the British steamer *Benlomond* was torpedoed by a German submarine. By a stroke of luck, Poon Lim found an 8ft-square (2.4m) life raft stocked with cookies, water, flares, and an electric torch. He also caught birds, small fish, and sharks to eat before being rescued by fishermen off the Brazilian coast—after spending 133 days alone at sea.

1945: On July 30, during World War Two, the USS *Indianapolis* was torpedoed in the South Pacific. Although around 900 of the men survived the sinking, they then had to endure nearly a week in the ocean fighting off attacks from sharks attracted by the blood and carnage. Although the sharks devoured the dead bodies first, many servicemen were eaten alive while awaiting rescue.

1973: When Maurice and Maralyn Bailey set sail from Panama in their yacht, bound for the Galapagos Islands, little did they know the terrible ordeal ahead of them. A wounded whale smashed a hole in their boat and they had to abandon ship. Grabbing some food supplies, they drifted on a life raft and small dinghy. Surviving at first on cookies for breakfast, peanuts for lunch, and a can of hot food at night, they then ate the turtles they had befriended. After a grueling 117 days at sea, the Baileys were picked up by a Korean fishing boat.

2002: Richard Van Pham left Long Beach, California, bound for the exotic island of Catalina, but a storm crippled his mast, engine, and radio. Although he drank rainwater and ate fish, birds, and turtles, he lost 40lb (18kg) while adrift in the ocean for 120 days. When rescuers found him off the Costa Rican coast, he was grilling a seagull using wood from his boat as fuel!

2005: In October 2005, three Mexican fishermen—Lucio Rendon, Salvador Ordonez, and Jesus Lopez—left the Pacific port of San Blas, Mexico, to go shark fishing. After running out of fuel, they were sucked into the North Equatorial Current and drifted for 5,000 miles (8,000km). Ingeniously, they made a sail out of blankets and fishing hooks out of engine parts, subsisting for 286 days on raw fish, seagulls, and sea turtles. By a stroke of good luck, they had fresh water to drink as it rained nearly every day (although they did have to keep bailing out their boat!). They were eventually spotted and rescued by a Taiwanese trawler off the Marshall Islands.

`Maritime moral:` Look out for hull-ramming whales and pray fishermen see you drift by in your boat!

SPECTACULAR
FEATS OF ENDURANCE

In 1992, Australian medical student James Scott was volunteering at a hospital in Nepal. Scott enjoyed trekking in the Himalayas in his spare time and set off on a trek just before Christmas. As the winter snows set in, Scott became separated from his friends. Lost and disorientated, he had only two chocolate bars, a notebook, and a copy of Dickens's *Great Expectations*. As his supplies ran out, he survived on snow and caterpillars. Amazingly, Scott was rescued 42 days after starting his spectacular journey.

The Sahara Desert is no holiday destination, but French adventurer Emile Leray decided to make the best of it. In 1993, he became trapped in the arid desert when his Citroen 2CV hit a rock and broke down. Leray decided to build a motorcycle using wreckage from the car. As his water and food supplies dwindled before his eyes, he worked non-stop for 12 days in the burning heat. Amazingly, Leray rode out of the desert on his self-built bike!

In 1997, mountaineers Sir Chris Bonington and Douglas Scott were descending Baintha Brakk—a mountain in Pakistan known as "The Ogre"—when disaster struck. Scott shattered both legs below the knee while abseiling down a rock face. Remarkably, he crawled down the mountain on his hands and knees! Even more amazingly, the helicopter taking Scott to hospital crashed on arrival—but he survived.

In 1994, when Italian police officer Mauro Prosperi ran an ultra marathon in the Moroccan Sahara, he found himself 186 miles (299km) off course in Algeria. Taking shelter for a couple of days in an abandoned mosque, he survived by drinking his own urine. He also drank blood from bats living in the mosque by cutting off their heads, mixing up their insides, and sucking everything out. After almost giving in to despair, Prosperi began walking again, eating raw snakes and lizards, before coming across an oasis and a Berber family who cared for him. He had survived an astonishing nine days in the desert.

In 1942, during World War Two, Robert "Jock" McLaren and Johnny Funk were both incarcerated in a Japanese prison. Determined to escape, the pair broke free. Island-hopping across the Pacific and pursued by the Japanese, they finally reached the Philippine island of Mindanao. By this time, McLaren had developed appendicitis. Having no alternative, he surgically removed his own appendix using a mirror and pocketknife, plus some jungle fibers to stitch up the wound.

ADVENTURES THAT WENT WRONG

In 1995, safari guide Paul Templer was attacked by a very angry male hippo, while leading a group of tourists down the Zambezi River. The hippo tried swallowing Templer head first! In an amazing display of courage and strength, he managed to escape the animal's jaws. Although the hippo attacked again, leaving Templer with multiple injuries, he somehow survived the vicious attack.

Aron Ralston was climbing in a Utah canyon when he got his arm trapped by a loose boulder. Stuck there for four days, Ralston realized his only chance of rescue was to amputate his own arm. Once he'd removed his arm, he hiked for several miles until he found help. His extraordinary tale of bravery and determination is depicted in the film *127 Hours* (2010).

Mont Blanc in the Italian Alps is famous for its frequent avalanches. As three British climbers were descending the mountain in 2013, an avalanche struck. Two of the climbers jumped to safety, but the third was caught in a terrifying wave of snow and ice. He managed to "swim" with the avalanche for 2,300ft (700m), remaining close enough to the surface to haul himself to safety as the avalanche came to a halt.

In July 1865, Edward Whymper and a group of companions reached the summit of the Matterhorn, a mountain that looms above Zermatt, Switzerland. On the way down, one of the group, Douglas Haddow, slipped and knocked four of the others to their deaths, including Lord Francis Douglas (son of the Marquess of Queensberry). The rope holding the men together snapped and they fell 4,000ft (1,200m) to an icy death. But the snapped rope saved Whymper and two guides from the terrifying fall. So shocked was English society by the tragic accident that Queen Victoria called for mountaineering to be banned.

SHOCKING
CANNIBALISM
INCIDENTS

Australian Katherine Knight was convicted in 2001 of stabbing her boyfriend John Price—and then eating him. Knight removed pieces of flesh from the corpse before cooking them with cabbage, baked potato, and pumpkin. Knight is now serving a life sentence in prison.

In 1972, a small plane carrying the Uruguayan rugby team crashed in the Andes Mountains, in Argentina, killing 29 of the 45 passengers. Nando Parrado and Roberto Canessa survived the plane crash and then heroically set off on foot in search of help, battling across the mountains for 10 days. Those left behind, desperate to survive, had no option but to eat their fellow (dead) passengers to get through the terrifying ordeal.

Alfred Packer was an American gold prospector and also a convicted cannibal. On February 9, 1874, Packer embarked on an expedition with five other people into the Colorado mountains. When he returned alone two months later, suspicions were aroused. Packer claimed he'd killed his fellow travelers in self-defense and been forced to eat their remains to survive. No one believed him. After signing two separate confessions, Packer was given a 40-year jail sentence.

Would you voluntarily visit a known cannibal? Well, Bernd Jurgen Armando Brande did just that, answering an online advertisement placed in 2001 by Armin Meiwes that read: "looking for a well-built 18 to 30-year-old to be slaughtered and then consumed." Meiwes first cut off Brande's penis, which he cooked and served for his victim, before killing him and cutting up the body. Meiwes ate the poor victim's body over a period of 10 months—he is now serving a life sentence in Germany.

In 2009, after accidentally killing his wife Dawn—by gagging and tying her up to stop her from drinking and driving—David Viens, who was a qualified chef, slow-cooked her body for four days. Viens apparently dumped his wife's remains in the bin, apart from the skull, which he hid at his mother's house.

CHEATING DEATH....JUST

In 2007, while walking with her husband, Jim, in Prairie Creek Redwood State Park, California, 65-year-old Nell Hamm fought off a mountain lion. As the lion wrestled Jim to the ground, Nell beat it with a log and tried stabbing it in the eye with a pen—the surprised cat fled the scene.

Unlucky Roy C. Sullivan, a US park ranger, was struck by lightning seven times in his lifetime. The odds of this happening are 22 septillion to 1! Roy even got hit when he was inside a ranger station. How unlucky can you be?

Ever been confronted by a black bear? Well, this is what happened to Gilles Cyr in October 2013 as he walked near Grand Falls, New Brunswick. As the bear's massive jaws gaped in his face, Cyr grabbed hold of its tongue and did not let go. Unbelievably, the bear hit out at Cyr to get him to release his grasp, but to no avail. Eventually, the bear ran off, leaving Cyr with only a few claw and bite marks.

OMG, it's a shark! In 1963, Australian Rodney Fox didn't panic when he was attacked by a great white shark while spear-fishing. Instead, he tried to gouge out the shark's eyes. As the shark then tore at his arm, Rodney put it in a bear hug before trying to swim to the surface to breathe. The shark chased after him, biting at his float line. Miraculously, the line snapped and Rodney managed to escape. His terrible injuries required 462 stitches, but he had beaten off a shark—and cheated death! (If this makes you scared to go in the sea, just remember: you are more likely to die from falling in a hole after digging sandcastles than you are from being eaten by a shark!)

Tsutomu Yamaguchi was a born survivor, narrowly escaping death by atomic bomb. Visiting Hiroshima on August 6, 1945, Yamaguchi was just stepping off a tram when the atomic bomb exploded about 2 miles (3km) away. Incredibly, he had survived the nuclear attack, but, unfortunately, he decided to go home to Nagasaki—just in time for the second atomic bomb to detonate 2 miles away again. Yamaguchi went on to live to the age of 93!

CHAPTER 6

OMG! IT'S

GLIMPSES INTO THE PAST

STRANGE BELIEFS
AND
HORRIBLE HABITS

The Romans used urine to clean their teeth and keep them sparkling white—we're assuming they used their own pee and not other people's!

The Ancient Egyptians would go into deep mourning and shave their eyebrows when a much-revered cat died.

The mighty Julius Caesar wore a laurel wreath to cover his increasing baldness.

When taking an oath in a court of law, Roman men would place a hand on their testicles. This is where we get the phrase: "to testify."

The Ancient Greeks believed
that gold was made from
water and sunlight.

! ! ! ! ! ! ! ! ! ! ! ! ! ! ! ! ! !

In the Middle Ages guests at a
wedding party would throw
sawdust at the bride and groom,
rather than confetti. Wedding
cake was also sometimes thrown
at the happy couple.

The Romans would add honey
and spices to wine, but this
popular beverage might also
have been flavored with resin
and even sea water.

MONARCHS...
BOTH MIGHTY AND MAD

Egyptian pharaohs had royal bottom wipers. This isn't just an eccentricity from the distant past, though, as later British kings, including Henry VIII, would appoint a Groom of the Stool to help them discreetly manage their royal excretions and ablutions.

On his death in 1087, William the Conqueror was too big to fit his coffin, so two soldiers tried to squeeze him in. Unfortunately, his stomach exploded. Nice.

Charles VI of France (1368-1422) believed he was made of glass. So, he refused to travel by coach—just in case he shattered into pieces. He wasn't called "Charles the Mad" for nothing.

Elizabeth I was the first person to own a flushing toilet in Britain. She also owned an incredible 2,000 dresses and 80 wigs. For some reason, she also put a tax on beards?!?

During the reign of English king William III (1650–1702), a garden fountain was used as a huge punch bowl. Want the recipe? Well, you'll need 560 gallons (2,546 liters) of brandy, 1,200lb (544kg) of sugar, 25,000 lemons, 20 gallons (91 liters) of lime juice, and 5lb (2.3kg) of nutmeg—oh yes, and a servant to row around in a small boat to fill up guests' glasses.

Prussian Frederick William I (1688–1740) thoroughly enjoyed military pursuits, but made sure that his special regiment of very tall soldiers were kept out of battle. Whenever he was unwell or depressed (which was quite a lot of the time), he would order a few hundred of them to march through his bedroom to cheer him up.

In 1862, the then Prince of Wales got a tattoo on a visit to Jerusalem during a royal tour—so starting a tattooing craze back home in Victorian England.

DEATH, DISEASE, AND THE ODD CURE

Egyptian dentists would tell patients to place half a hot, freshly killed mouse in their mouth to cure bad breath. But then, they also thought powdered mouse brains made a good toothpaste!

The Ancient Egyptians were very medically advanced, but did have some odd cures—for example, they treated blindness by grinding up a pig's eye with antimony (a type of metal), red ocher, and a little honey before pouring the concoction into the patient's ear!

Historical cures for the Black Death included eating a spoon of powdered emeralds, consuming some rotten treacle—as long as it was 10 years old—and bathing in urine.

Medieval treatments for many diseases involved praying to patron saints for a cure. St. Fiacre, a 7th-century Irish monk, was the patron saint of hemorrhoids. If you were afflicted with this condition and the praying hadn't worked, then medieval physicians would insert a red-hot iron into your bottom. Ouch!

! ! ! ! ! ! ! ! ! ! ! ! ! ! !

Heard of a clyster? Well, this long metal tube with a plunger at one end was used to perform enemas in the Middle Ages. Pretty similar to today's enemas, but with one big difference—thinned boar's bile or vinegar might be pumped into the sufferer's anus instead of warm, soapy water.

i i i i i i i i i i i i i i i i

In Victorian England, people would pay to have photographs taken of deceased loved ones as a sort of keepsake. These were known as *memento mori*. Quite often, living family members were photographed with the dead relative, who would be dressed in their best and nicely "posed" for the camera.

The Victorians used electrotherapy to cure all sorts of ailments, from gout to muscle weakness. These electric shocks didn't work, however, leaving most patients with burn injuries.

PAST
PUNISHMENTS
AND EXECUTIONS

If you were found guilty of stealing cattle in Ancient Egypt, you would be taken to the top of a cliff and thrown down onto a sharpened pole. OMG!

In 16th-century England, the friends of heretics who were condemned to burn at the stake were sometimes allowed to hang a small bag of gunpowder around their necks to speed up the process.

A Roman method of execution involved the unfortunate victim being sewn into a sack containing a live dog, monkey, cockerel, and snake.

In the 18th century, men known as baby-getters would visit prisons and, for a fee, impregnate female prisoners who were condemned to die, in order to obtain a stay of execution for them.

> The guillotine was last used in France on September 10, 1977— that is, when the first *Star Wars* film came out.

In 1386, a pig was tried and executed by public hanging in Normandy, France, for the "murder" of a baby. Strangely, the villagers dressed the pig in clothes. The animal became known as the famous Sow of Falaise.

Unbelievably, a female Asian elephant that performed in Sparks World Famous Shows circus was hanged in Tennessee in 1916 for killing a cruel trainer.

WACKY

WAR FACTS

Just one shot was fired in the 1784
"Kettle War" between the Netherlands
and the Holy Roman Empire. Quite
unbelievably, it hit a soup kettle!

During the American Civil War, General Joseph
Hooker wanted to keep his men happy, so he made
sure his troops were accompanied by a group of
willing ladies—that is why the word "hooker"
is used as slang for prostitute.

The Anglo-Zanzibar War of
1896 is the shortest war
in history—lasting only
38 minutes.

In 1938, you could obtain gas-resistant baby carriages (i.e. sealed-in perambulators)—just in time for World War Two, then.

Fashion designer Hugo Boss manufactured the uniforms for the Nazis.

" Soldiers in World War One urinated on their boots to soften the leather. "

All British tanks since 1945 have been fully equipped with tea-making facilities.

The first bomb dropped by the Allies on Berlin during World War Two killed the city zoo's only elephant!

Hand grenades sent to Resistance fighters in Norway during World War Two were hidden inside fish cakes!

In one day of heavy fighting during the 1942 Battle of Stalingrad, Russia, a local train station changed hands from Soviet to German control and back again 14 times in six hours.

The Germans plotted to kill Sir Winston Churchill with an explosive device disguised as a bar of chocolate.

In World War Two, the Americans tried to train bats to roost in enemy territory and explode bombs —at night, presumably.

Authors'
ACKNOWLEDGMENTS

First and foremost, we would like to
thank Cindy Richards and the lovely
team at CICO—including Sally Powell
and Pete Jorgensen —for asking us to
write and create another book. As
always, a very special thank you goes to
Pete Jorgensen who always sees the
potential in our projects. Thanks, Pete!

In the interests of accuracy, the
information in this book has been
cross-referenced over as many different
sources as possible. However, inevitably,
as you journey back into the near and
distant past, it can become more difficult
to substantiate some facts and statistics.
So, sincere apologies in advance
for any errors.

O.M.G

So that's the end!

FOR NOW.....